Benjamin
May your blessings be many
may your conflicts be few
may your Impact be lasting
may your Legacy bring honor
To your name

LEGACY

WHAT'S YOURS GOING TO BE?

NORM KOBER
BILL EVERETT

WE OWN IT, WE CONTROL IT, WE
DECIDE WHAT IMPACT OUR LEGACY
WILL HAVE ON THE FUTURE.

Norm Kober

Legacy - What's yours going to be?

with Bill Everett

ISBN: 978-1-48359-176-6

Table of Contents

INTRODUCTION

I have been blessed to have lived long enough and have been associated with Chick-fil-A long enough to have learned that there are some things that may not be clear to a younger person. It has little to do with intelligence or ability - time and experience are the only teachers of these lessons. One of the lessons I've learned is that heroes do not die. Heroes are those individuals whom we look up to and honor and desire to imitate with our own lives. Long after they are gone from this life, they continue to live on in others. As long as someone, somewhere, is being impacted by the life and example of their hero, then that hero lives on. I have been an operator for many years now and some of my heroes have been other Chick-fil-A Operators and staff.

Truett Cathy, the founder of Chick-fil-A is one of those heroes. I believe Truett has influenced me more than anyone else. He and these other Operators made a deep and lasting impression on me and I know that each of them influenced the lives of many other people in positive life changing ways. Don't get confused, I'm not talking about making money or running a successful business. I'm talking about having a successful, happy, fulfilling, and significant life. In the next few pages, I will share some of what I learned and how I learned it in a short story about four funerals. I hope that as you read the story you will be able to see what I saw in these four men, my heroes.

At some point someone might ask you what is it that you want to accomplish with your life or career. Another way of thinking about it is what would you like other people to say about you after you are no longer around. For me, I hope that someone would say "he was a hero of mine." This isn't my ego and it's not that I want to be idolized. Instead it's that I want someone else to have a better life because of what they might have learned from me or that I served them somehow and made a significant difference in their life.

My hope is that if you are reading this you will give serious thought to what you want to accomplish in life. I hope it includes service to others, because if it does you will learn that serving others can bring happiness and reward beyond your imagination.

Norm Kober

FOUR FUNERALS

I'm older now than I've ever been. That may sound a little obvious to you but when you've lived as long as I have…it gives perspective. You get to enjoy the legacy you are leaving a bit more than when you were younger and still building it. Hopefully I'm wiser and more compassionate and caring than I've ever been but getting older gives you the ability to look back on your life and see how the decisions you made, the people you impacted helped to craft that legacy that eventually you will leave when you pass from this world to the next. However, the longer you live the more you will say goodbye to friends and loved ones, and those who impacted your life, as they *slip the surly bonds of earth.*"* I've been to more funerals than I would have liked by this time but let me tell you what I learned by attending four of those funerals.

All four were funerals of people that left a powerful legacy and made an impact on many lives. The first funeral was for a young man that I met thirty-seven years ago. At the time I was in the process of opening my first Chick-fil-A restaurant in Brownsville, Texas at Sunrise Mall. In those early days of Chick-fil-A there was no Support Center staff to handle all the things that go into opening a new unit. Somehow Jimmy Collins & Truett Cathy managed to negotiate a lease, build a unit, find an operator willing to take on the responsibility of that unit and set the wheels in motion for an opening with a staff of twelve, including family. This staff consisted of full timers and a few young men that were either working part time while attending college or were between college and a full time career choice.

That's when I met Roger Clapp the first time. Roger was one of those young men that was doing a very big job with very little training or experience. Roger had been working for Bubba Cathy and was asked to go to Brownsville as construction was finishing and the equipment and package arrived. Roger travelled to Brownsville alone and took control of everything. Yes, everything. That was 100% of setting up a unit, equipment supply, vendors, everything.

As I remember, Roger did all of this in less than a week. He was my 100% support staff from the time I started training which was a 4-day long weekend spent in Atlanta - some of it at Southlake mall and 2.5 days at the original home office at 801 Virginia Avenue in Hapeville, Ga. There, I learned everything I was going to need to know about running a business for myself, but not by myself, as Truett liked to say. We became very good friends even though we only got to see each other at the annual Chick-fil-A seminar. Roger was only with me for one week, four days before opening and three days after opening but his impact on my life continues to this day.

As those first few years of our friendship passed our lives were changing dramatically. Frances and I were having children and my family was growing. I had been asked to move to a new unit and one of my first hired team members became the youngest Chick-fil-A operator at my previous unit. Roger had settled in Memphis where he was originally from and had finally met and married a wonderful young lady. He also had been selected to run a Chick-fil-A restaurant in that area. At that point in time it seemed we both had the world at our feet and life was great and God was blessing us more than we deserved.

And then I got the news Roger had died suddenly and unexpectedly.

Rogers's funeral was painful; I had never lost someone that was so important to me. Truett attended the funeral and took a small group of operators out to a restaurant after the service was over. I don't remember much from that day except that Truett was there with those of us that loved Roger. He was sharing and ministering to us even if we didn't know it at the time. You see Truett loved Roger as I did. It became apparent to me that Roger and I, and all the other operators and staff were like family to Truett. In fact, he treated everyone as he would treat his own family and for the rest of his life, that never changed for him.

The day I attended Truett's funeral at the Support Center in Atlanta is when I started to put together the significance of what I was seeing there that day exactly 35 years to the day that I had opened my first unit with Rogers help - Sept. 10, 1979 to Sept. 10, 2014.

What I experienced at his funeral or as I would describe the celebration of Truett's greatest achievement, because I knew that he was in the presence of God by that time – was profound for me.

Each of us will stand in judgment someday in front of God and if we have lived a life pleasing to God in service to him and others we will hear "Well done my good and faithful servant", welcoming us to be with Him for eternity. I know this will be my greatest achievement and I'm confident that Truett was welcomed by God to be with Him.

That day at the Support Center, Truett's legacy was shared by operators, staff, family, friends and a community that loved him the same way I loved Roger. Truett had done so much for so many because it was what God expects of us. It has little to do with business or what we have. It's that we serve others with whatever we have, regardless if it's only a little training and experience, or all the resources that Truett came to have at his disposal. The Support Center was filled as was Truett's church and several other venues - as I understand it - with people who wanted to pay respect to him.

Pay respect – that means we recognize that person has lived a life of significance, a life that in some way deserves our respect. It may seem obvious to any that know Truett's story that much of his life, if not all of it was spent making sure that others were taken care of, or that he was making sacrifices to make the lives of others better. In his life we can see lasting examples - a large prosperous enterprise, a children's home; Lifeshape and Winshape ministries; and all that those encompass as well as the less obvious impact his legacy will have for generations to come.

Truett was Rogers's inspiration from a young age and he lived out those same values that Truett built his life on. I hope you are beginning to see the connection and what I remember that day at the Support Center. Let me tell you about the other two funerals that I connect to this story.

In 1979 Billy Roberson opened a Chick-fil-A Restaurant in San Angelo, TX a few months after I opened my first unit. Billy remained in San Angelo his whole time as an operator and passed away unexpectedly a few years ago. I attended Billy's funeral in San Angelo and as I drove home afterwards I had time to think about the events and the experience of that day. I realized that I needed to send a letter of thanks to the Chick-fil-A staff at the Support center that attended Billy's funeral. I've inserted the actual letter here to share the impact of the events of that day:

I wanted to thank you all, for taking the time to show respect for what Billy Roberson spent 34 years building. It meant a lot to me that Chick-fil-A Inc. would take the time to show that respect. As I mentioned to some of you after the service, the time that we spent hearing about Billy's life and how he had impacted so many lives could never be matched by a seminar presentation about what our role as Operators should be about. The profit/income we generate from sales is how we make a living, not how we make a life. It struck me as I looked at everyone in the church and heard the stories from the pastor and Billy's son that he had built a legacy that anyone would be proud of, and that legacy is much more valuable than the money he may have earned over the years. Where have we heard: "a good name is worth more than silver and gold?"

San Angelo is one of those places that you might pass through on your way to some place of interest, but you wouldn't be heading there without a really good reason. As I drove the 6 hours home I could only think about what I had experienced that day. Billy built a personal brand and the Chick-fil-A brand by doing what Truett told us would work best – the Golden rule. Billy did it in San Angelo for 34 years. He didn't move to Dallas or Dimmit, or Dime Box or Dilly (all Texas cities) or some-place where the income opportunity might have appeared to be brighter…he built it right where he started.

I believe Billy understood that the Operators real role and opportunity for success is to add value to others and to our com-munities. We heard many examples of Billy treating others with honor, dignity and respect and his love for and concern for others was obvious. Billy built the Chick-fil-A brand the old way, the way it has been built by many that attended his funeral, those Operators that sat behind you and around you, those with the thin and graying hair, some a little over weight and hard of hear-ing. Billy didn't need or count on fancy prepackaged marketing events like Daddy daughter date night, and I don't believe he did many, if any, back stage tours at his DTO**. Those things might be fun for some and help tell who we are but they are not a sub-stitute for Operators loving on their people and their communi-ties. Billy's life and how he operated his business is a testament to what has worked for many in the past and will always work best. Mandy – Billy's Business Consultant - mentioned that on her last *visit with Billy before his stroke he was excited about the future and had specifically mentioned his intention to be number 1 in sales for Chick-fil-A by knocking me out of that position. I'm sure after seeing Billy's little DTO that he surely would have already led all Chick-fil-A in sales, if he had had a full size unit, as he led in the DTO category. I might suggest that if Operators are looking for a place to visit on an excellence tour, staff might suggest a visit to that little DTO in San Angelo while it still exists. Operators often look to other Operators that are doing well in sales and profits and tend to look for secrets and systems and little tricks of the trade that give them an edge in the business. Instead, I think a bit of time spent sitting on the picnic table outside of that little DTO in San Angelo wearing a Chick-fil-A name tag would surely lead to conversations with those that you met there. They would probably talk about Billy and how he made a difference in the lives of so many, and isn't that what excellence is really about and what the real secret is to making this thing work. Thanks again for being there and for all you do. Norm Kober 2013*

The fourth and final funeral that I attended took place a year later. In 2014 I received the sad news that another long time operator from Tyler, Texas, Ed King had passed. For as long as I had been an operator, I had many occasions over the years to get to know Ed, often over the thirty plus years, Ed and I would end up at Chick-fil-A functions together, primarily due to the fact that both our last names began with a K. So it seemed like we were either in a line waiting or seated together during a Chick-fil-A activity. Ed was another of those persons that spent a lifetime serving others. Besides myself, his funeral was attended by a large group of both older and younger operators, CFA staffers, Dan and Bubba Cathy, and most of the executive committee. Just like in Billy's case, the church was completely filled with family, friends and team members both current and former, plus countless people that Ed had touched in his community in some way.

After the church service the ladies of the church served a lite snack and coffee during that time, and I believe most of the Chick-fil-A folks wore their name tags. There was a constant stream of people that Ed had touched/impacted over the years that would come up to the Chick-fil-A staff or operators and want to share a story about what Ed meant to them. There was usually a story about a time that Ed had gone out of his way to do something for them or the group they belonged to. It became obvious that he loved to help people. All of these men were not marketing when they offered help to a person or group. They were living a life of generosity, of service, and a life that would be pleasing to God.

The four funerals that I attended were of people that helped shape me. Each of these men understood that serving others was what God wanted them to do. Rogers's impact on me was earlier in my career, because of the way he helped me (a new guy) get started. He began setting the ground work for my career with Chick-fil-A and my life from that point on. Helping another by sharing whatever skill and talent or passion you have is powerful. Billy, Ed, and Roger exemplified what you can do by applying the values that Truett modeled for everyone at Chick-fil-A and for anyone that had the opportunity to get to know him.

As I write this I'm reminded of a message that was delivered to the Chick-fil-A family years ago at the annual seminar by Rev. R. L. Patterson, who told us the little known story of Shamgar from the bible. There is only one verse in the whole bible about Shamgar. If you will read Judges 3:31 you will learn that Shamgar had amazing results by doing just three things. Here is the list:

#1 - Start where you are.

#2 - Use what you have.

#3 - Do what you can.

And even more amazing is that each of us have the same starting point as Shamgar. If you will do what Shamgar did - start where you are, use what you have and do what you can - then you too can have amazing results in your life and in your business. Each of the four men that I've been talking about did as Shamgar did and yes, each had amazing results. It has been an honor to have known and learned from these four men and I will never forget any of them.

LEGACY

Legacy is sometimes described as what a person leaves behind. A legacy is not your material things, and it is more than an emotional thing. It might be described as the way the world sees what you have accomplished. Just as a ship leaves a wake behind that travels out and affects everything it touches, a person affects everyone they come in contact with in life. The effect of a ships wake depends on the force or power that the ship is propelled by. The effect of a person's legacy is also dependent on the force or effort that is put into creating a legacy. It can be positive or negative. The important things for each of us to understand is:

We leave an impression or mark on everyone we come in contact with in life.

That mark that we leave can be a positive or a negative mark

We each have the power to determine if our impact or mark will be positive or negative.

I believe that there are a couple of ways that the impact of your legacy is determined. We can just go through life on a day to day basis without making a decision about what we want our legacy to be. This tends to be most people's approach to life.

OR

We give thought to what we would like our legacy to be, and make a plan that will help to ensure we make it happen.

We own it, we control it, we decide what impact our wake, our legacy, will have on the future.

If you are in the first group, you may want to stop reading now and decide to move on with your life, and not invest your time and energy in building a positive legacy. But if you are interested in what significance your actions in life have, then continue reading and you might learn a few ideas on how to create a lasting positive legacy with your life.

The neat thing about that legacy is that it's an area of your life that only you have the ability to decide what happens. Like most of the really important things in life each individual makes the decisions that have the most profound results. By this I mean that if you think about your life—no one else has the ability to make your most important decisions, like what you will do for a living, who you will spend your life with, or who you will serve in this life - will you serve God, or will you serve only yourself? Legacy fits in this category of the most important decisions of your life and only you get to make the choices that determine what it will be.

Now if significance and a positive legacy are important to you then it's time to get to what makes it happen. Planning a positive legacy is easy but making it happen is anything but easy. I have learned that the first and most important step is choosing a set of values that will create a positive legacy. For me this is something I learned from the founder of Chick-fil-A, S. Truett Cathy. If you knew Truett you would know some of the values that he built his life and a successful business on — Values like Faith, Integrity, Industry, Morality, Honesty, Generosity, Optimism, Courage and Excellence.

This would be a good list of values for anyone to adopt. Truett's life is a testament to what can happen if you elect to embody these values. If you haven't heard his story or the Chick-fil-A story, then I recommend that you find one of his books or watch the video in Chick-fil-A's orientation materials and learn more about him. Now comes the hard part, you must not only choose values that will lead to positive results, but you must also live out those values - everyday - in every part of your life. This is what we call embodying the values.

That's right, you read correctly. That's why it's the hard part. Living out these values, in every part of your life, every single day is not easy. Why? Because life is full of temptations. Temptation often causes us to fall short of living out or embodying our values. Many times I've joked and said that I can resist anything...except temptation. Usually people laugh because most people are like me and know that we are human and weak. This is where faith and prayer can help.

In every area of our life we need to embody the values. Our dealing with people both in our families and in the public must be guided by honesty, integrity and morality. If we try to cheat in any area it will eventually catch up with us. Eventually is the key word here. I believe I will have to answer for my actions. You will never be able to have a positive impact on others if you are not seen as trustworthy. Trustworthiness is an accrued asset. By this I mean you build it up like an investment that gains interest. It takes time and stewardship. Like investments it takes discipline and you must be adding to the principle if you expect the interest to add up to a meaningful amount. It's the same with trustworthiness.

Finally, let me highlight four of those important values that should be the cornerstone of your legacy...and they are centered in your work life. They are optimism, courage, excellence, and generosity. Let me explain why these are very important in the work that a person does.

It takes a positive attitude to look for possibilities and not obstacles, this is optimism. When we identify an opportunity that may seem too big to tackle, courage will serve you well in problem solving and finding the solutions. I define courage as being unafraid of failure knowing that most victories come by learning from previous failures. And victories prepare us for even bigger future challenges.

Excellence is a goal for anything we do. Would you like to be known for anything less? Do you believe anyone will ever recommend a person that is just average in what they do? Would you hire or welcome a person into your organization that had being average as their goal? Truett Cathy has said that average is being the best of the worst or the worst of the best.

Everyone can appreciate craftsmanship in anything, it doesn't matter if it's a handmade item, a well written book, a great athletic performance or brain surgery. Excellence is what's respected in what people do. Last but not least, is generosity. Why do I include generosity as a cornerstone of legacy building?

Generosity can be defined as giving unselfishly, giving of what you have, your time, your talent, your treasure (what makes you special) to the world. Treasure may be resources, but it also might be a spiritual or intellectual gift or it might be the ability to pray for someone else's needs above your own. The amazing thing about giving generously is the giver always receives a huge gift by giving.

You have to experience it for yourself to truly understand the concept of giving unselfishly. You might like to think of the following names when you thing about generosity and legacy. Mother Teresa, Mahatma Gandhi, Bill Gates, and Truett Cathy all have been generous and have left a tremendous legacy shaped by their generosity towards others.

What will your legacy be? If you are reading this, it is likely that you are young and probably just starting your adult life. This is a great question to ask yourself now as you begin to make the choices for your life now. If you will do this then many years from now when you story is told, when you are remembered, and when you look back on your life you will see the wonderful legacy that you left to others and the positive impact your life had on this world.

VALUES TO LIVE BY

Values are what we give worth or merit to and they can be anything from human traits and characteristics to more tangible things like a college education. Usually they are passed down from our parents or family but they are also picked up as we go through this life, and as we grow and develop as human beings. Values are very important in that what we value will affect our behavior and our success in this life and usually set you on a path for this life. So for those who value college education it is likely that they will get a college degree which will then impact their job potential and their future.

On the next few pages are a short list of values that we feel are important and necessary to be successful in both relationships as well as results in the business world. They are by no means the only values that are important but a short list of some that we believe under-gird the life that has a positive impact on others.

Neither are they in any order of importance. They are important values nonetheless and you can find each of them in the Bible. In other words, they are biblical values or values that God has deemed as important to live a life pleasing to Him. As you read on we encourage you to think of ways that you can apply and embrace these values for your own life.

TRUSTWORTHINESS

When my father was growing up many contracts between individuals were no more than a simple handshake and the bond of each other's words. Sadly, those days are gone. People do not trust each other and for good reason: they have been burned in the past by others that they thought they could trust. It's an amazing statistic that the most un-trusted group of people today in our society is our government leaders, the top in the land.

Trustworthiness is an accrued asset. By this I mean you build it up like an investment that gains interest. It takes time and good stewardship.

Trustworthiness springs from the ability to keep your word, no matter the cost, along with a persistence to maintain it. Another way of saying this is a person who is trustworthy is a person that you can depend upon to keep their word to you.

Psalm 15:4 tells us that the person who pleases God is someone who *"keeps his word even to his own hurt."* What this means is if you said yes to something, no matter how difficult the circumstances are to fulfill it, you are going to keep your word and do it. **Even if it costs you something in the process.**

Yet being known as an untrustworthy person will have much greater cost to you in the long run.

The interesting thing about trustworthiness is that you cannot be trustworthy except in the eyes of others. People trust you because over a period of time you have proven to be a person of your word, or as Jesus said, *"let your no be no and your yes be yes, anything other than this is evil…"* So when a trustworthy person says they will have an action item done at a certain time then you know that they will have it done by then. They may lose sleep over it but they will do everything in their power to meet that deadline.

Trustworthy people can also be trusted to keep confidences. That's because they have a high moral and ethical standard and if they are asked to keep something confidential then you can rest assured that they will not let it slip out. It's also the little things that you expect that trustworthy individuals do, like being on time for work, maintaining a sharp image and having good personal hygiene. At Chick-fil-A being trustworthy is a high value. Without people to depend upon you cannot run a restaurant well. It really does not matter what business you are in, without trustworthy and dependable people you will not have much of a business.

A person who is known to be untrustworthy will have few, if any, healthy relationships and find it very difficult to get ahead in this life. Often the legacy that they leave behind is one of regret, shame, and broken relationships. Today, choose to be a trustworthy person. Let your yes be yes and your no be no and slowly and surely you will find the reputation of being trustworthy will make a way for you in the eyes of your supervisors, your friends and family.

INTEGRITY

Integrity and trustworthiness are two peas in the same pod. A person is trustworthy usually because they are a person of integrity. Integrity comes from the same root word that we use in math for integer and it means whole. The dictionary defines integrity as the quality of being honest and having strong moral principles; moral uprightness. Secondarily it is the state of being whole and undivided.

By combining these two definitions: when we say a person has integrity what we mean is that they are a person who is not double minded but lives in a state of honesty and moral uprightness. Using a computer term, another way of saying it is that people who are integrous are WYSWYG people. That is, they are "What you see is what you get" kind of people. They don't have hidden agendas, they are true to themselves and true before others. They are who they are whether in public or private. But more than that they are people who have a strong moral and ethical code and stick with it even when it's difficult to do so or when popular opinion is moving the other way.

This doesn't mean that they don't grow, change or develop. As all healthy people do they will grow in understanding, develop as people and even change their opinions about things. But they do it with integrity.

The book of James tells us in James 1:8 that the *"double-minded person is unstable in all their ways."* This is the outcome of someone who lacks integrity: they become unstable in every area. Instability is not something you can build anything on including a successful life and career.

Work at becoming a person of integrity. It doesn't come easy or sometimes even naturally. When we are pressed from the outside to do or say something that is not integrous for us you have a choice at that moment. You can choose to continue to build a life of integrity, one small choice after another, or you can take the easy way out and go with the flow.

As the saying goes:

> *Sow a thought, reap an action*
> *Sow an action, reap a habit*
> *Sow a habit, reap a character*
> *Sow a character, reap a destiny.*

> \- Seneca

I can promise you that years later when you look back on your life you will be glad that you chose to be a person of integrity.

HONESTY

"God...loves the company of those who keep their word."

- Proverbs 12:22

In the United States we honor those whom history has said were honest. From our first president George Washington (as one legend tells us could not tell a lie about chopping down a cherry tree) to the 16th president, Abraham Lincoln who was nicknamed "Honest Abe" we consider honesty in a person to be a very high value. The phrase "honesty is the best policy" was originally penned by Sir Edwin Sandys, one of the founders of the Virginia company of London that established the first colony of settlers in Virginia in 1606. You could say that from the very beginning of our country honesty has been a high value.

Isn't it true that we're always looking for honesty in someone? Whether it's the doctor who has bad news or the mechanic who is diagnosing the problems with your car, honesty is sought after by people. In normal circumstances there is almost no instances where there is a good reason to be dishonest with someone else.

Dishonesty can be exaggerating the truth or leaving out details that twist the truth. You can lie by withholding information or not saying anything. Deceit comes in many forms.

Most of us do not consider ourselves to be liars. But lying starts by telling little "white" lies. Lies that we think really do not hurt anyone. And we begin to build an immunity towards honesty. Little by little a person can move towards dis-honesty without thinking about it and before you know it you have become a dishonest person.

No one trusts someone who is known to be dishonest and that kind of a reputation will badly impact your ability to be successful in this life. So make an effort to always be honest in all your dealings with others. As you go through life you will find that: Honesty is always the best policy!

MORALITY

The dictionaries definition of integrity includes moral uprightness. Today the issue of what is right and what is wrong is coming under increasing attack. Often we hear someone say don't judge me when they do something wrong. Yet the Bible is often very clear about what is right and what is wrong in God's eyes.

When Leaders have moral failures it grieves the community around them. Whether it's a business or a church community or even a neighborhood— moral failure tears the fabric of the community. The deeper issue, when it comes to right and wrong is not so much the behavior. Behavior stems from what is inside a person. It is only the symptoms of a deeper issue within. Jesus put it this way:

And he (Jesus) said, "What comes out of a person is what defiles him. For from within, out of the heart of man, come evil thoughts, sexual immorality, theft, murder, adultery, coveting, wickedness, deceit, sensuality, envy, slander, pride, foolishness. All these evil things come from within, and they defile a person." Mark 7: 20—23

Every person in this life has a sense of what is right or wrong. Almost universally, murder is considered to be bad no matter what people group, ethnicity or country you go to.

Lying and stealing are still considered to be wrong by most people around the world.

To use a term within the construction industry every person in this world has a "plumb line" regarding what they think is right or wrong. A plumb line is a line from which a weight is suspended and it determines the exact direction towards the center of the earth. This helps in building house that is straight and true and not crooked. If a builder just eye balled it and said that looks straight by the time he was finished, he would find walls that were crooked and joints that did not match. It is not the line itself that is the causal agent but the earth's gravity. The plumb line is simply the thing that tells us where the center of gravity is and therefore what is straight up and down. Each of us has an internal plumb line which tells us what is straight (right) and what is crooked (wrong). Usually this is embedded in us from the way we were raised, by our parent's view of what is moral and by the influence of others around us. But even before that there is an innate sense of right and wrong that God puts within each of us – like a plumb line. Our plumb line can be affected by others around us for good or for bad. 1 Corinthians 15:33 tells us *"Do not be deceived: "Bad company corrupts good morals."*

Morality is a difficult thing to discuss due to a shift in our cultural mores. What one person thinks is right may be different than what another person thinks. As many people think today *"what is true for you may not be true for me."* This is partially due to the belief that there is no real truth that one can embrace or believe outside of your own personal experience.

This view or philosophy has invaded our culture and has damaged it significantly.

What can be done? Jesus himself contradicts this view when he says *"I am the way, the truth, and the life. No one comes to the father except through me."** The answer is we have to look to a greater authority outside of ourselves to help find the truth. If you are going to have a straight plumb line in this life your center of gravity should be what God says is right and wrong. God's word, the Bible, is how we find what God thinks about what is right and wrong. It is the center of gravity for our lives and how we know if our plumb line is straight.

The Bible often gives us Gods view on morality. Sometimes it is evident as in the Ten commandments that God gave to Moses or it is subtler and takes some study to determine it. Either way, if you want to be a moral person then make Gods word the center of gravity for your internal plumb line. The Bible also tells us that when you become a Christian God gives you his Spirit who will lead and guide you in the way that you should go. The Spirit will never contradict the Bible - so make it your plumb line for moral behavior in this life.

INDUSTRIOUSNESS

That's a big word isn't it? One that we don't use much in our normal conversation. Yet it is key to being successful in this life. We can define it as simply working hard and being diligent and devoted to what we do. At Chick-fil-A industriousness is also key to being a success and was handed down to us by our founder, Truett Cathy, who embodied industriousness and a work ethic that at times seems legendary.

Because Truett's original restaurant, the Dwarf Grill was open 24 hours (except on Sundays) Truett was known to even sleep on a bunk at the Restaurant in the early years and when he would hear a car and the sound of wheels crunching the rocks as they pulled into the parking area, he would get up out of bed and fix whatever meal they asked for. That model of industriousness has been handed down to us as we endeavor to live out that legacy as well. Being industrious is a biblical value. The Bible tell us that *"Whatever you do, work heartily, as for the Lord and not for men."* Colossians 3:23

Everyone who has been successful in this life has been a hard worker, devoted to their profession. Even people who are highly gifted must work hard at their craft to be successful. One of the great geniuses of the last century was Thomas Edison (the inventor of the light bulb among other things). People would ask Edison about his profound intellect and how that had made him into such a great and famous inventor. His now famous reply *"Genius is one percent inspiration and 99 percent perspiration,"* rings out to each of us like a gauntlet thrown down and he himself lived it out often working 20 hour days to accomplish his inventions.

Nothing ever comes to one, that is worth having,
except as a result of hard work.
- Booker T. Washington

Here's the great thing about industriousness. No matter how smart or gifted you are, if you work hard, you will do well in this life. You may not be the genius Thomas Edison was (few are) but you can be industrious and develop yourself and rise above the others who don't put in quite as much devotion as you do to your job.

No one ever accomplished anything of worth in this life because they haphazardly applied themselves to doing it. Industriousness and hard work can make up much a person may lack in other areas.

OPTIMISM

Having a positive and optimistic outlook will go a long way to smoothing that path that we walk on in this life. If the glass is half empty, all the time and you look at everything from a negative viewpoint then life will not only be difficult for you but for those who work with you.

The bible gives us a principle on how to do this:

Finally, brothers, whatever is true, whatever is honorable, whatever is just, whatever is pure, whatever is lovely, whatever is commendable, if there is any excellence, if there is anything worthy of praise, think about these things. Philippians 4:8

This is not a denial of reality. Being overly optimistic and not living in reality can be just as bad. If things are tough or hard, then admit it but don't stay there. An optimistic viewpoint says "sure, some things have gone wrong, but I'm not staying there. I have a plan to move forward from this point or mistake."

The 1930's and early 1940's was a dark time in the world. The 1930's were marked by the great depression and by late in the decade World War 2 had begun and the world sank into one of the greatest and most terrible wars that history has ever known. To counter that negative sense of what was happening

Johnny Mercer wrote a song that exemplified and encouraged people to stay positive, even in those difficult hours.

Here are some of the lyrics:

> *You've got to ac-cent-u-ate the positive and*
> *E-lim-in-ate the negative.*
> *And latch on to the affirmative*
> *Don't mess with Mister In-Between*
>
> *You've got to spread joy up to the maximum*
> *Bring gloom down to the minimum*
> *Have faith or pandemonium's*
> *Liable to walk upon the scene*

Maintaining a positive attitude even in the valleys of this life will help to make it more endurable. But what if I make a mistake or even fail? How do I maintain a positive attitude when I mess up?

Minister and motivational expert John Maxwell likes to say it this way: everyone fails...but the successful person is the one who gets up and brushes themselves off and learns from that failure. In a sense they are people who fail forward. What failing forward means is what the optimistic person does: they get up from that failure or mistake, learn from it and then move forward in their life, not living in regret or getting stuck in that moment but pushing on to higher and greater goals.

Attitude is more important than you think when it comes to success in life. As Motivational Speaker Zig Ziglar liked to say: your attitude will determine your altitude. If you keep a positive attitude the sky's the limit. Having a positive outlook on life in general will open doors and smooth out rough roads for you. To help develop a positive attitude, hang out with positive people. Avoid people who are always bad mouthing others or talking negative about life.

One of the best ways to gain a positive attitude is to read the Bible and understand how much God loves you and values you. More than anything else knowing you are loved and valued gives you a sense of esteem that will increase your positivity ratio. So work on maintaining a positive outlook on life and having a positive attitude in whatever you do. If you do, things will go better for you.

COURAGE

This life requires courage. The timid person will find the rigors of this world to be daunting. Sometimes in your life you will find moments that will take significant courage to face. Great fear may come upon you, as it does everyone, but when you do face those moments in your life you will have a choice to make. Will I push on despite my fear or will I cave in and allow fear to dominate me and the decisions I make in this life. Courage is not the lack of fear. Courage is the ability to move forward despite the fear that we may have.

One of the best ways to have courage is to know that you are doing the right thing and know that God is with you. The Israelites were facing fearsome enemies as they began to enter the promised land and fear was rampant in the community. Even Joshua their leader, was wondering how they were going to do this. In the midst of their concern God spoke through an angel to Joshua and the leaders of Israel: *Be strong and courageous. Do not be terrified; do not be discouraged, for the Lord your God will be with you wherever you go.* Joshua 1:9

Though you may never be in the situation where lives depend upon your courage you will come across times in your life where courage is needed. A more common situation that you will find yourself in is when you will have to choose what you believe or know to be the right thing, yet everyone or everything is going against you and you feel significant pressure to cave in. This is where courage comes in and says no matter the repercussions I will do the right thing.

Some years ago a friend of mine was told by his supervisor to hide files from a federal agency doing an audit for the company. Instead of doing so he told his supervisor no and was shortly relieved of duty and fired a few days later. It was a painful experience and he was humiliated by it. A couple of days later he began the process of preparing his resume to begin the arduous task of finding a new job. Unbeknownst to him a company contacted him within a few days and offered him a better job with better pay and benefits.

Whether or not that happens in every case it is always better to be courageous and do the right thing no matter the potential consequences. Ultimately we answer to God in this life for our actions and He's got your back, so be courageous!

EXCELLENCE

A good definition of excellence is doing the best you can with what you have. Approaching a task or assignment with the mentality that I am going to do this to the best of my ability. The Bible tells us the following:

"So whether you eat or drink, or whatever you do, do everything for the glory of God." - 1 Corinthians 10:31

We have had this scripture up on top of our registers for all our team members to see. This helps them understand that ultimately they are not working for their boss so much as they are working for God and should work accordingly.

If you are working for God then, should you not work your best and do things with as much excellence as you can. At Chick-fil-A being excellent in our operations is foundational to what we do. It does not matter how well you do customer service and connect with the community if you do not have excellence in how you operate the restaurant.

How many of us would fly on a plane where the reputation of the pilot was one of mediocrity or go to a surgeon for an important procedure that was known to not be the best. Absolutely not. We want the best when it comes to our lives. We want those who are excellent at their craft or jobs. Why should it be any different whether you deliver the mail, drive a truck or raise cattle for a living or work at Chick-fil-A? When work and life are done with excellence everyone benefits.

Truett Cathy, the founder of Chick-fil-A liked to ask his staff as well as the operators of the restaurants, "*Why not your best?*" Why not? What is keeping you from giving your best effort at whatever you put your hand to?

How can you become excellent in what you do? Train and develop yourself. Go to school to learn greater skills. Find a mentor who can help train you. Work hard at what you learn and be conscientious about how you do your work. Remember, whatever you do, do for the glory of God. If you do, then your gifts and skills will eventually make a way for you.

GENEROSITY

Generosity can be defined as giving unselfishly, giving of what you have, your time, your talent (what makes you special), and your treasure to others.

Someone might think it's strange to have this value as part of living a successful life. But if you look at the lives of those individuals who have done well you will find that most of them were also very generous with what they had.

People who gain a lot of wealth often find that there isn't anything particularly satisfying about simply getting a lot of money. A number of them, including Truett Cathy find much more satisfaction in giving away and investing in others with the money that God has given them.

A life of generosity far outweighs the temporary pleasures that money can bring and you do not have to have much wealth to be a generous person. The Bible tells us that Jesus lived a life of generosity towards others.

In all things I have shown you that by working hard in this way we must help the weak and remember the words of the Lord Jesus, how he himself said, 'It is more blessed to give than to receive.'" Acts 20:35

Generosity is more than giving money. It is a way of life that is giving to others in innumerable ways. You may be able to help people with your gifts and abilities. The simplest way of giving to others is with your time. Be generous towards others in different ways, with your gifts, with time, money and energy and you will have true riches in this life.

FAITH

Someone once said *"you gotta have faith, brother"* and the reality is that faith does have real impact on a person's outlook in this life which in turn affects their potential. In other words, faith creates a positive outlook in life which others see and respond to. A person who does not have a positive outlook tends to affect people around them negatively. Having faith in yourself and your God given talents and gifts will help to propel you forward to excellence and success.

We've already written about this in our chapter on optimism. Faith is more than having an optimistic or positive outlook on life. Faith is that quality that comes from a deep understanding that God loves us and wants the best for our lives and has a purpose for our lives and has given gifts, abilities and talents to either expend on ourselves or on others.

"Now faith is being sure of what we hope for and certain of what we do not see." Hebrews 11:1

Having faith in this life starts with the understanding that there are greater things that we cannot see and more wonderful than we can imagine. We cannot touch faith. We cannot see, smell or touch love, though we can feel loved by someone. Faith, much like love, is outside of our five senses.

The bible tells us that people may fail us but God is faithful. Having faith in God and his word to lead, guide and direct our paths is key to being successful—though the bible's definition of success is much deeper than how people typically define success. It is more about positively impacting others around you, whether your family, your children, or your co-workers. It is more in line with leaving that legacy behind you of people whose lives have been enriched simply by knowing you.

The Bible tells us that faith is actually a gift given to us by God.[1] In this world where people hurt one another and there is suffering and pain in this life Faith is sorely needed. God is not to blame, he warned us in the Garden of Eden millennia ago that sin would bring destruction and pain. But humanity has continued to rebel against God. That is why God sent his son Jesus Christ to this world some 2000 years ago. So that we might have life and hope and salvation from our sins. Jesus said it this way:

"For God so loved the world that he gave his only begotten son that whosoever believes in him will have everlasting life." John 3:16

This kind of faith, given to us by God, is the starting point for everything else we've been talking about in this little booklet. Today, if you have never done so, why don't you invite God into your life and give him complete control over the direction of your life. It starts with what you think about the most important person who has ever lived – Jesus Christ.

We started this book with legacy. What will be your legacy on this planet? On your family? On the others that have known and loved you? One day you will die, as all do. Nothing goes with you. What will you leave behind you? A legacy of love and kindness, serving others with the gifts God gave you? Helping those less fortunate than you? Embodying the values in this little booklet will take you a long way towards leaving a positive, life affirming and faith filled legacy on all those around you. You can build a positive legacy with your life, start right now, with what you have and begin to do it. May God bless you as you begin a wonderful legacy in this life!

NOTES:

Four funerals

(High flight by John Gillespie Magee Jr.)

** Drive thru only*

Morality

*John 14:6

Faith

[1] Romans 12:3